Creation to Christmas
around
THE JESSE TREE

Creation to Christmas
around
THE JESSE TREE

Written by: Pamela Nelson

XULON PRESS ELITE

Xulon Press Elite
2301 Lucien Way #415
Maitland, FL 32751
407.339.4217
www.xulonpress.com

Unless otherwise indicated, Scripture quotations taken from the New Century Version (NCV). Copyright © 2005 by Thomas Nelson, Inc. Used by permission. All rights reserved.

Printed in the United States of America.

ISBN-13: 9781545639559

The Jesse Tree is sure to make the stories of Creation to Christmas come alive and will become a treasured family tradition for years to come.

The daily ornaments can be made as a fun project, or miniatures can be found at a nearby craft or hobby shop. For ornaments that are difficult to find, try making them out of clay or use pictures mounted on small pieces of wood.

Following is a list of corresponding ornament ideas:

Table of Contents

Creation

Day 1

In the beginning, God created the sky and the earth.

Genesis 1:1

In the beginning, the earth was empty, and God said, "Let there be light"; and God separated the light from the darkness. There was morning and evening the first day.

On the second day, God created the sky.

On the third day, God created the dry land and the sea, and all the plants and trees on the earth.

On the fourth day, God created the sun and the moon to rule over the day and night.

On the fifth day, God created the sea animals and the birds.

On the sixth day, God created all the animals on the earth, and the first man and the first woman.

On the seventh day, God was very happy with all that He had made, and He rested.

The Fall of Adam and Eve

Day 2

So she took some of its fruit and ate it. She also gave some of the fruit to her husband, and he ate it.

Genesis 1:1

God named the first man Adam, and He named the first woman Eve.

God put the man and the woman in a special garden He called Eden.

God said, "You may eat the fruit from any tree in the garden, but you must not eat the fruit from the tree which gives the knowledge of good and evil. If you ever eat fruit from that tree, you will die!" (Genesis 1: 16-17)

One day, an evil snake came into the garden and asked Eve why she didn't eat the fruit on that tree.
He told her that if she ate the fruit, she would be just like God.

Eve believed the snake and ate the fruit, and gave some to her husband, Adam.

God was very sad and told Adam and Eve that they had to leave the beautiful garden.

The Flood

Day 3

After seven days Noah again sent out the dove from the boat, and that evening it came back to him with a fresh olive leaf in its mouth.

Genesis 8:10-11

Adam and Eve had a son named Seth and eight generations later Noah was born. This was 1,500 years after Adam and Eve left the beautiful garden. God told Noah to build an ark, because a great flood was coming.

Noah and his three sons worked very hard building the ark.

When Noah was six hundred years old, he, his wife, and his sons and their wives, and two of every animal went into the ark.

The Flood came, and only Noah and his family, and the animals with them, survived.

When the Flood was done, Noah sent out a dove, and the dove came back with an olive branch in his beak.

Noah knew then that the water was almost dry.

He waited seven days until he knew it was safe for his family to go outside.

Noah and his family came out of the boat and thanked God.

God put a rainbow in the sky to remind them that He promised He would never again send a great flood like that to destroy the earth.

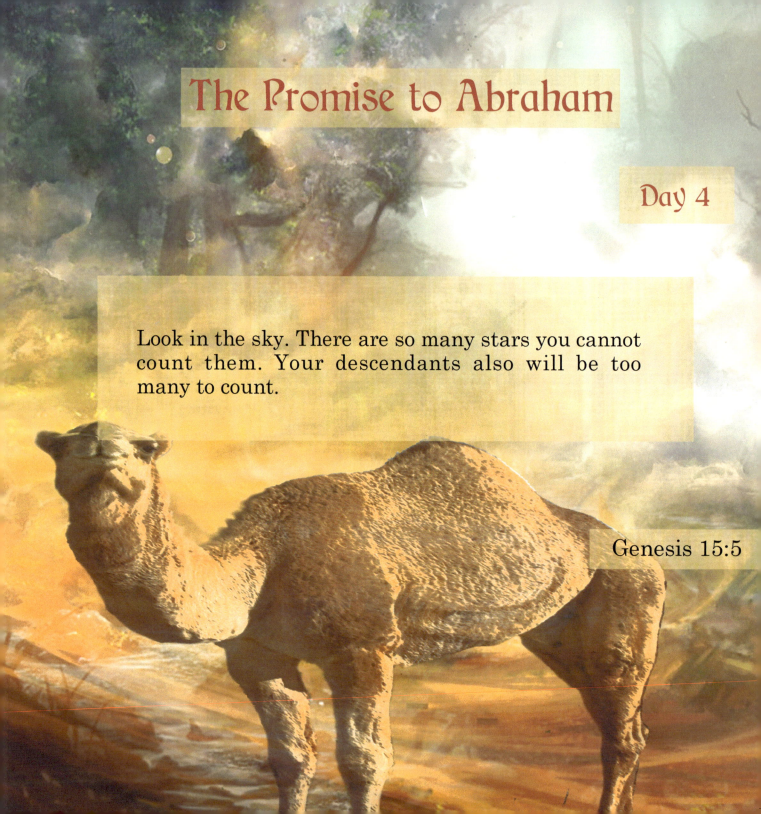

The Promise to Abraham

Day 4

Look in the sky. There are so many stars you cannot count them. Your descendants also will be too many to count.

Genesis 15:5

It was five hundred years after the Great Flood that God spoke to Abram and his wife Sarai. He told them to go to the land of Canaan.

God told Abram he was going to change his name to Abraham, because he was going to have many children (as many as the stars in the sky).

God told Abraham that he was going to change Sarai's name to Sarah, which means "The Princess."

God told Abraham and Sarah that they were going to have a son.

Abraham and Sarah were very old, and they thought this was funny because they didn't know how two old people could have a baby.

Isaac and the Lamb

Day 5

Abraham answered, "God will give us the lamb for the sacrifice, my son."

Genesis 22:8

At the top of Mt Moriah is a special place named Golgotha.

Abraham and Sarah had a son and named him Isaac.

God told Abraham to take Isaac up to the mountain called Mt. Moriah and to sacrifice him.

Abraham believed God would take care of him, no matter what.

When Abraham was just about to sacrifice Isaac, God said, "Look in the bushes, and you will find a lamb.

Sacrifice the lamb instead of Isaac."

The lamb took the place of Isaac.

Joseph's Coat

Day 6

He made Joseph a special robe with long sleeves.

Genesis 37:3

Isaac had a son named Jacob.
Jacob's family called themselves Israelites.
Jacob had a son named Joseph.
Now, Joseph was born when his father was very old.
His father loved him very much, even more than his brothers.

Jacob made a very special coat for Joseph.

Joseph had eleven brothers.
His brothers did not like him, because they were jealous that their father loved him so much.

One day, Joseph's brothers sold him as a slave to some people going to Egypt.
They told their father that Joseph had been eaten by wild animals.

Joseph had a very hard time in Egypt, but after many years, he became a great ruler there.

Back in Canaan, Joseph's family didn't have enough food to even survive.
They went to Egypt, looking for a way to get food.
When Joseph saw that his brothers needed help, he forgave them and helped them.

Moses

Day 7

She put the baby in the basket. Then she put the basket among the tall stalks of grass at the edge of the Nile River.

Exodus 2:3

Another five hundred years had passed since God spoke to Abraham. At this time many Israelites were living in Egypt, but there was an evil king in Egypt.
He made life very hard for the Israelites.
He said that when a baby boy was born, the baby must die.

A woman named Jochebed had a baby boy, and she hid him as long as she could.
When the baby was three months old, she made a basket and put the baby in it.
She put the basket at the edge of the water.

The daughter of the king came to the river to take a bath.
She saw the basket and looked inside.
When she saw the baby, she decided she wanted to take him home, but she needed someone to take care of him.

The baby's sister, Miriam, was watching all of this and she said, "I can get someone to help you." She hurried away and brought back Jochebed to help.

The king's daughter named him Moses, which means "out of the water."

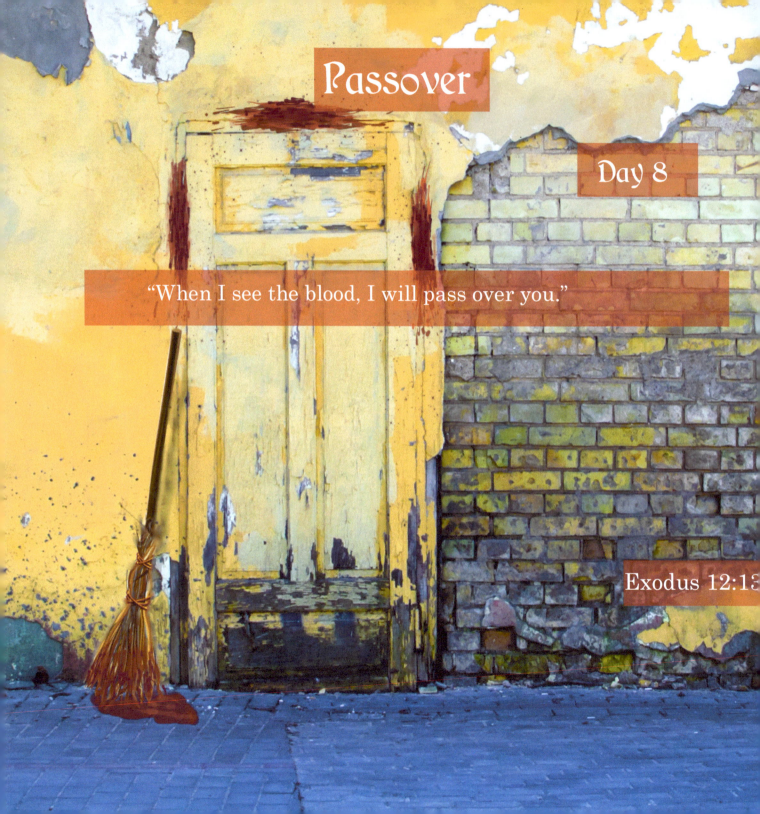

Passover

Day 8

"When I see the blood, I will pass over you."

Exodus 12:13

God told Moses and his brother Aaron to tell each family to get one lamb that was perfect in every way.
This lamb was going to be used for something very special.

Moses and Aaron told the people to take the blood from the lamb, and put it on the top and the sides of their front doors.
That night, they should eat the lamb with some special bread and some special spices.

God said that in the evening, He would be going through the land and that all the firstborn children and animals would die.

He said He would "pass over" any house that had the blood on the door.
No people or animals would die there.
He said that nothing terrible would hurt them.

This was the first Passover.

The Ten Commandments

Day 9

He gave him the two stone tablets with the Agreement written on them, written by the finger of God.

Exodus 31:18

When Moses was eighty years old, God said that He wanted to talk to him on Mt. Sinai.

Moses went up the mountain to talk to God.

The people heard a trumpet and loud thunder and saw lightning and smoke. They were so afraid that they shook and stood far away from the mountain.
God told Moses many important things about how the people should live that day.
God wrote all the things he told Moses on stone tablets for Moses to take back to the people.

When Moses came down from the mountain, the people were all misbehaving.
This made Moses so mad that he threw down the stone tablets and broke them.

God was not happy about this, and so Moses had to go back up the mountain a second time.
Moses took two new stone tablets up to the mountaintop, and God wrote the Ten Commandments on them again.
Moses took the two new tablets and put them in a very special box that God told Moses to make.

The Promised Land

We went to the land where you sent us, and it is a fertile land! Here is some of its fruit.
But the people who live there are strong. Their cities are walled and very large.

Numbers 13:28

God promised Moses that He would give the Israelites a new land.

Moses sent twelve men to go look at the land that God promised them.

They saw grapes that were so big, it took two men to carry them back.

Ten of the men said they were afraid to go to the land, because the people were so big and they were afraid of them.

Two of the men (Joshua and Caleb) said, "We should go to the land because God told us to go."

The people listened to the men that said they were afraid, and so the people didn't go.

This made God sad, because they didn't believe He would take care of them.

The people had to wait another forty years before they could go to the land.

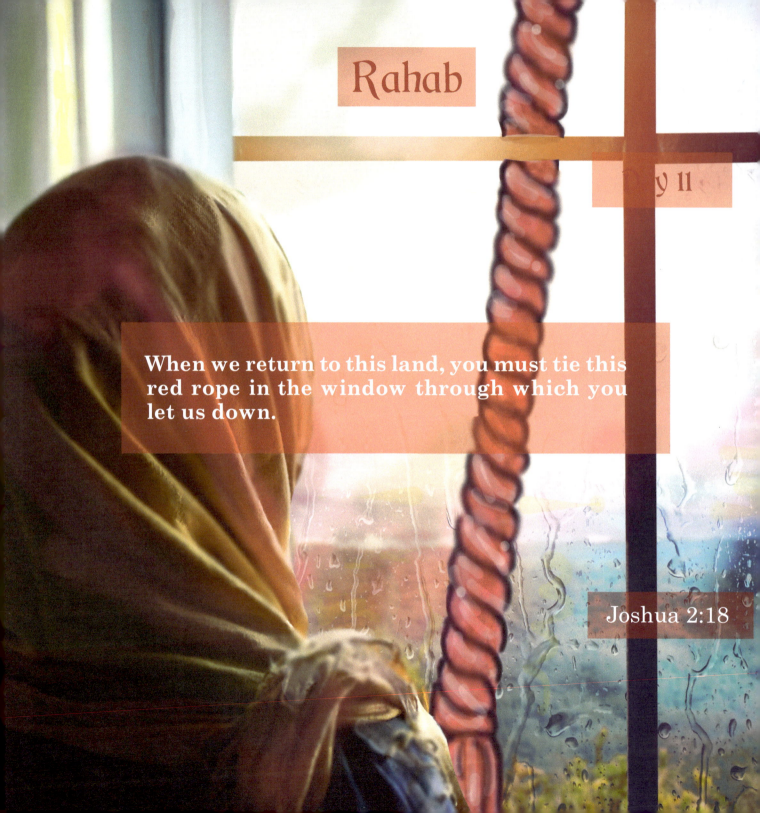

Rahab

Day 11

When we return to this land, you must tie this red rope in the window through which you let us down.

Joshua 2:18

Joshua sent two men to spy on Jericho.

While they were there, they needed to hide from the bad king.

There was a woman in Jericho named Rahab, and she helped the two men hide.

She asked the men if they would be kind to her family, when they came back with their army to attack the city.

The men told her to hang a red rope from her window, so they would know which house belonged to her.

When the Israelite army attacked Jericho, they kept Rahab and her family safe.

Ruth and Boaz

Abraham answered, "God will give us the lamb for the sacrifice, my son."

Ruth 1:16

Did you know Ruth wasn't an Israelite and yet she is listed in the lineage of Jesus?

Another three hundred years after God gave Moses the Ten Commandments, a woman named Ruth lived in Moab.
Ruth did not know God at first.
She was not an Israelite.

Ruth's husband died, and she loved his mother (whose name was Naomi) very much, so she went to Bethlehem with her.
Ruth said to Naomi, "Where you go, I will go. Where you live, I will live. Your people will be my people, and your God will be my God." (Ruth 1:16)

Ruth and Naomi didn't have much food, so Ruth gathered the leftover wheat in the fields, after the workers of the fields were finished.
There, she met a man named Boaz.

Boaz's mother was Rahab.

Ruth and Boaz got married, and had a son named Obed. Obed had a son named Jesse, and Jesse's son was King David.

David

Day 13

"But I come to you in the name of the Lord All-Powerful, the God of the armies of Israel! You have spoken against Him. Today the Lord will hand you over to me, and I'll kill you and cut off your head……Then all the world will know there is a God in Israel!"

I Samuel 17:46

When David was a boy, he was a shepherd in Bethlehem.
He took care of the sheep.
That is where he learned to use a slingshot.

A giant named Goliath came to fight the army of David's people.

All the men were afraid to fight the giant.

David was just a boy, but he wasn't afraid.

Goliath laughed at David.
Goliath said to David, "Do you think I am a dog that you came to fight with a stick?"

David killed Goliath with only one rock in his slingshot.
He did not even have a sword in his hand, and Goliath was covered from head to toe in full body armor.

Root of Jesse

Day 14

A new branch will grow from a stump of a tree: so a new king will come from the family of Jesse.

Isaiah 11:1

Three hundred years had passed since David was a boy, when a man named Isaiah began to write about things that were going to happen in the future.

He was a prophet.

He wrote about a new branch coming out of a stump of a tree called the root of Jesse.

The new branch means a new king will come, and he will be from the family of Jesse.

Isaiah said this new king will be wise and fair, and strong and good.

Isaiah wrote about many things that were going to happen that hadn't happened yet.

The Lion and the Lamb

Day 15

Then wolves will live in peace with lambs, and leopards will lie down to rest with goats.

Isaiah 11:6

Isaiah wrote that someday God will make a new earth.

He wrote that in the new earth, a child will have a lion as a pet.

This new earth will be like the one that Adam and Eve lived in.

Animals will not hurt or destroy each other or people.

Prince of Peace

His name will be Wonderful
Counselor,
Powerful God,
Father who lives forever,
Prince of Peace.

Isaiah 9

Isaiah tells more about what it will be like when God makes a new heaven and a new earth.

He said there will be a new king.

This new king will be a good king, and a loving king, and a fair king.

He will be the Prince of Peace.

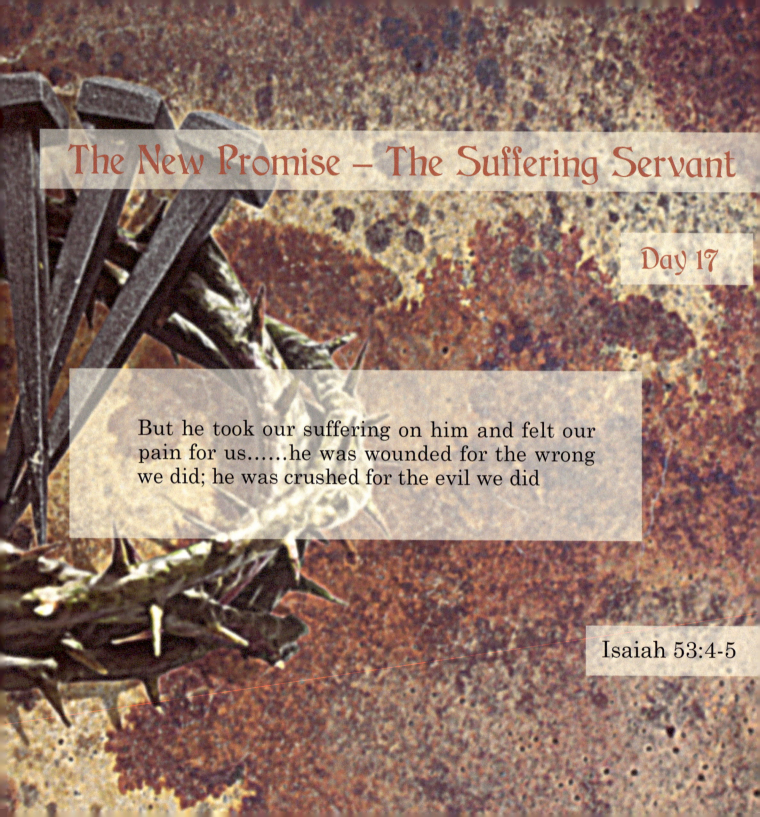

The New Promise – The Suffering Servant

Day 17

But he took our suffering on him and felt our pain for us……he was wounded for the wrong we did; he was crushed for the evil we did

Isaiah 53:4-5

God saw that people couldn't keep the rules of the Ten Commandments.

This made God sad, because He really loves people and wants to spend time with them.

God told Isaiah that He had a plan to take care of all the bad things that people do, so He can be with the people He loves forever.

Isaiah wrote about someone who was hurt very much and had a lot of pain, but he didn't say a word in his pain.

He said that this person never did anything wrong, but that he had all of this pain because he loved his people so much.

He said this person took the punishment that his people deserved.

Bethlehem

Day 18

But you, Bethlehem, though you are too small to be among the army groups from Judah, from you will come one who will rule Israel for me. He comes from very old times, from days long ago.

Micah 5:2

Another prophet named Micah wrote about the king of Israel being born in Bethlehem.

He said this king comes from very old times, from days long ago.

This king has been around since the beginning of creation.

He said this king would bring peace.

The people were very confused about who this king would be that has been alive since the beginning of time.

Josiah Finds The law

Day 19

Josiah did what the Lord said was right.

II Kings 22:2

Another one hundred years went by when a boy named Josiah was made the king. He was only eight years old.

Josiah's father wasn't a good king and didn't let the people worship God.

Josiah wanted to worship God.
He sent some men to the temple to clean it, and they found an old scroll that had been lost for a long time.
When Josiah opened the scroll, he realized it was the word of God.

He told the people about the scroll, and they started to worship God again.

The Passover had not been celebrated for a very long time. King Josiah began to celebrate the Passover again.

After King Josiah died, his sons were made kings. His sons and the people did not follow after God or listen to Him.

The king of Babylon attacked the people. He set the temple on fire and broke down the walls of Jerusalem. He took the people to Babylon and made them slaves once again.

The Fiery Furnace

Day 20

Look! I see four men walking around in the fire. They are not tied up, and they are not burned.

Daniel 3:25

Shadrach, Meshach, and Abednego said they would not worship any other god except the real God.

They had a king that said if they didn't worship his gods, they would have to be thrown into a fiery furnace.

They didn't care, and so they were tied up and thrown into the furnace.

The fire was so hot that it burned the soldiers that threw them into the fire.

What happened next was very surprising.

The king looked into the fire, and he saw four men.

They weren't burned at all, and they were walking around.

He said the fourth man looked like the son of God.

He ordered the three men to come out of the fire.

He said from now on, no one is allowed to say anything bad about the God of Shadrach, Meshach, and Abednego.

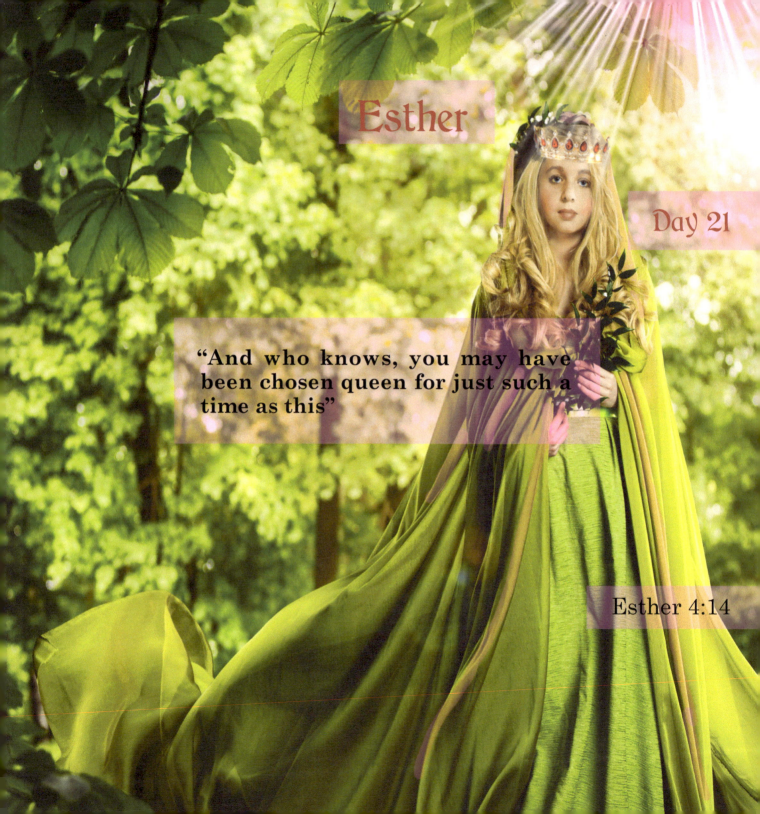

Esther

Day 21

"And who knows, you may have been chosen queen for just such a time as this"

Esther 4:14

Esther was an Israelite that lived with her cousin Mordecai in Syria.

The King of Syria was looking for a new queen.
He wanted all of the most beautiful girls of the land to come before him so he could choose one of them to be the new queen.
Mordecai told Esther that she should go before the king.
Esther did just that and amazingly, the king chose her.

The king did not know that Esther was an Israelite.

The king had an important man named Haman that told the king all about the things that were happening in the land.
Haman did not like Mordecai, and he told the king that Mordecai was bad and that Mordecai and all his people should die.
Mordecai told Esther all about Haman's plan. He told her that maybe this was why she was chosen to be the queen.
Esther had a plan of her own.

She invited the king and Haman to a dinner at her house.
When they came to the dinner, she told the king about Haman's plan and that Mordecai's people were her people.
She asked the king if he would please not kill all of her people.

The king agreed with Esther and decided that the bad things that Haman wanted to do to her people would actually be done to him and his people.

Return to the Land

Day 22

"May God be with all of you who are His People. You are free to go to Jerusalem and build the temple of the Lord, the God of Israel, who is in Jerusalem."

Ezra 1:3

The Israelites disobeyed God so many times that they were sent away to other lands to be slaves.

Finally, about two hundred years after the days of Josiah, Cyrus, the king of Persia, said the Israelites were free to go back to their own land.

The Israelites were so happy to finally be able to go back to their land.

They started to rebuild the temple and the wall around Jerusalem that all the bad armies before had torn down.

Angels Appear to the Shepherds

Day 23

Then a very large group of angels from heaven joined the first angel, praising God and saying, "Give glory to God in heaven and on earth, let there be peace among the people who please God."

Luke 2:13-14

One night, some shepherds were taking care of their sheep.

An angel appeared to them, and they were very afraid.

The angel said, "Do not be afraid; I am bringing you good news."

The angel told them that their savior had been born that night in Bethlehem; and that they would find Him wrapped in pieces of cloth, just like the cloths they wrapped newborn lambs in.

The shepherds were so excited that they quickly went to Bethlehem where they found Jesus.

They told Mary and Joseph all about what the angel said.

When they went back to their sheep, they were praising God and thanking Him for everything they had seen and heard.

It was just as the angel had told them.

The Star

When the wise men saw the star, they were filled with joy. They came to the house where the child was and saw him with his mother, Mary, and they bowed down and worshipped him. They opened their gifts and gave him treasures of gold, frankincense, and myrrh.

Matthew 2:10-11

Some wise men traveled a very long way to Bethlehem, because they saw an unusual star in the sky.

They followed the star because they wanted to worship Jesus.

The star that they followed led them to the place where Jesus was.

They brought Him gifts, and they bowed down and worshipped Him.

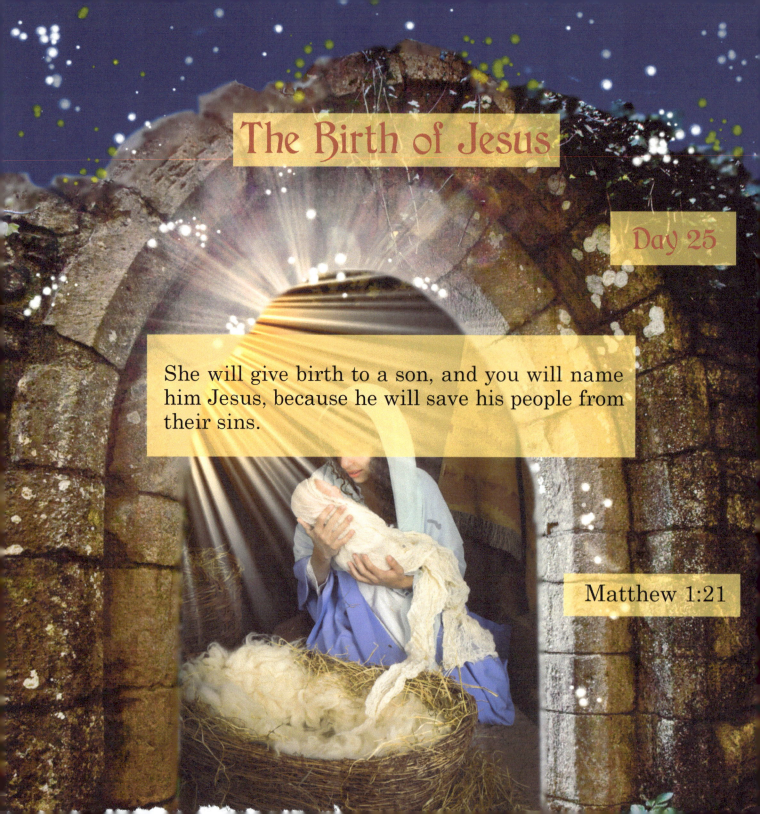

The Birth of Jesus

Day 25

She will give birth to a son, and you will name him Jesus, because he will save his people from their sins.

Matthew 1:21

An angel appeared to Joseph in a dream and told him that Mary was going to have a baby boy.

The angel told Joseph what to name the baby.

The angel told Joseph to name Him "Jesus," which means "God with us," because this baby boy was actually God.

Jesus was born in the town of Bethlehem, just like the prophets said so many years before.

CPSIA information can be obtained
at www.ICGtesting.com
Printed in the USA
LVHW071324131118
596934LV00005B/114/P